Searchlight BOOKS™

World Traveler

Travel to

France

Christine Layton

Lerner Publications ◆ Minneapolis

For Penelope

Consultant: Jessica Lynne Pearson, PhD, Associate Professor of History, Macalester College

Lerner Publications Company
An imprint of Lerner Publishing Group, Inc.
241 First Avenue North
Minneapolis, MN 55401 USA

For reading levels and more information, look up this title at www.lernerbooks.com.

Main body text set in Adrianna Regular.
Typeface provided by Chank.

Map illustration on page 29 by Laura K. Westlund.

Library of Congress Cataloging-in-Publication Data

Names: Layton, Christine Marie, 1985– author.
Title: Travel to France / Christine Layton.
Description: Minneapolis : Lerner Publications , [2024] | Series: Searchlight books - world traveler | Includes bibliographical references and index. | Audience: Ages 8–11 | Audience: Grades 4–6 | Summary: "France is one of Europe's most important cultural and economic centers. Explore the country's geography, government, people, and much more"— Provided by publisher.
Identifiers: LCCN 2022038344 (print) | LCCN 2022038345 (ebook) | ISBN 9781728491622 (library binding) | ISBN 9798765603826 (paperback) | ISBN 9798765600672 (ebook)
Subjects: LCSH: France—Juvenile literature.
Classification: LCC DC17 .L39 2024 (print) | LCC DC17 (ebook) | DDC 944—dc23/ eng/20220817

LC record available at https://lccn.loc.gov/2022038344
LC ebook record available at https://lccn.loc.gov/2022038345

Manufactured in the United States of America
1-53101-51111-2/10/2023

Table of Contents

Chapter 1

GEOGRAPHY AND CLIMATE

France is the largest nation in western Europe. Wild boar run through green forests near ancient castles and busy towns. The smell of pastries and bread flows from cafés. Tourists come from around the world to visit France.

Land

France lies between Belgium to the north and Spain and Andorra to the south. To the east, France borders Germany, Italy, Luxembourg, Monaco, and Switzerland.

The Atlantic Ocean and the Bay of Biscay form its western border. The English Channel sits to the northwest, and the Mediterranean Sea forms the southern border.

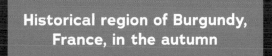

Historical region of Burgundy, France, in the autumn

Sheep graze in Normandy, France

Plains cover most of northern and western France. More plains dot the center and south. The Pyrenees mountains rise to the south. The Alps stand along the border of France, Italy, and Switzerland. Mont Blanc is the highest point in the Alps and in Europe. It is 15,771 feet (4,807 m) tall. The Loire is the longest river in France. The Seine flows through Paris, the capital city. Both rivers flow northwest through the center of France.

France's natural resources include coal, iron, and timber. Farmland covers more than half the country. Crops grow well in the rich soil. People fish along the coast.

LAVENDER FIELDS, PROVENCE

Must-See Stop:
Côte d'Azur

Côte d'Azur means "bright blue coast." This area of France has beautiful beaches and clear, blue water. Towns perch on cliffs that rise from the sea. Côte d'Azur is a popular tourist destination. Hotels, restaurants, and nightclubs line the beaches. Farther inland, tourists visit the Ecrins and Mercantour national parks.

Étretat, a coastal village in France

Climate

France has a mild climate but is experiencing more heat waves because of climate change. In the south near the Mediterranean Sea, the weather stays warm year-round. Average summer temperatures are around 77°F (25°C), and winters are mild. France is cooler in the north. The average temperature in January is about 43°F (6°C). Summers average only 60°F (16°C). Rain blows in from the Atlantic Ocean. The average rainfall on the west coast of France is more than 50 inches (127 cm).

Chapter 2

HISTORY AND GOVERNMENT

People have lived in France for more than one hundred thousand years. Cave paintings show life in early France. People hunted animals, built homes, and made art.

In 1200 BCE, Europe was home to the Celts. These groups of people shared language, religion, and customs. Two major groups of Celts, the Britons and the Gauls, lived in the area that would become France. Ligurians, Iberians, and other smaller groups also lived in the area.

Early France

In 50 BCE, the Romans conquered the lands controlled by the Britons and Gauls. The Romans called the land Gaul. The Roman Empire ruled Gaul for about five hundred years. Roman rulers spread their culture, language, and religion. Only small areas of Indigenous Celtic culture survived.

ROMAN AQUEDUCT, LANGUEDOC

Charlemagne

The Franks took over Gaul around 500 CE. They renamed the land Francia. By 771 CE, King Charlemagne ruled most of western Europe. Charlemagne died in 814 CE, and the empire split into five parts. For the next five hundred years, rulers fought for control. By 1453, France had established its modern boundaries.

The French Revolution

For centuries, France was ruled by a monarchy. The country fought many expensive wars, including helping support the American Revolution. In the late 1700s, King Louis XVI and members of the ruling class also spent huge amounts of money on themselves. To refill the treasury, the monarchy forced the French people to pay high taxes. Most French people worked hard to make a living. Drought and sickness made life even harder. Many French people did not want the monarchy to continue.

In 1789, people across the country came together to start the French Revolution. They broke into a fortress called the Bastille. They stole weapons. Throughout France, people fought against the people in power. By 1792, King Louis XVI, his wife, and thousands of people on both sides of the conflict were dead.

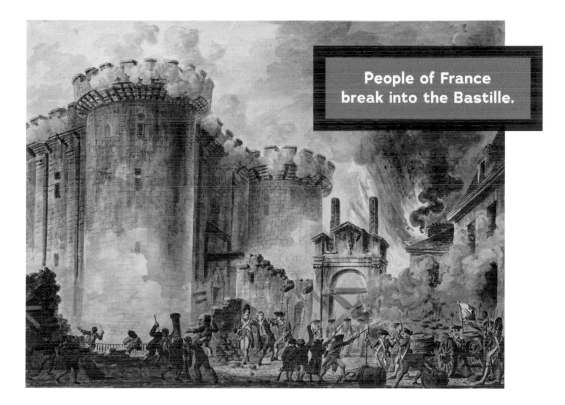

People of France break into the Bastille.

Must-See Stop:
Palace of Versailles

King Louis XIV ruled France from 1643 to 1715. He turned a hunting lodge into a grand palace. The Palace of Versailles celebrated the king's power and wealth. The palace became the official home of French kings in 1682. In 1837, the palace became a museum to preserve France's royal past. The palace sits on 2,000 acres (809 ha) of land. Beautiful gardens cover the grounds. Nearly every inch of the palace is filled with art and decoration.

This painting shows Napoleon crossing into the Alps on horseback.

After the revolution, French general Napoleon Bonaparte ruled the country. He crowned himself emperor in 1804. He led the French army to invade other countries. In June of 1812, Napoleon invaded Russia. But Napoleon lost hundreds of thousands of soldiers to winter weather, hunger, and disease. After Napoleon lost power in 1814, the monarchy returned for a short time. But by the end of the nineteenth century, the French Republic finally replaced the monarchy. In the new republic, most French men were able to help choose leaders. Women in France were not given the same right until 1944.

French president
Emmanuel Macron

Government

France has a president, a prime minister, and a group of high-ranking officials called a council of ministers. Citizens of France elect the president. The president is the head of the country's executive branch. The president chooses the prime minister, the country's second in command. The council of ministers, also chosen by the president, enforces laws. France also has a parliament made up of representatives elected by the people. The parliament creates the country's laws.

Let's Celebrate:
Bastille Day

Bastille Day is a national holiday celebrated each year on July 14. The holiday marks the fall of the Bastille and the start of the French Revolution. French kings used the Bastille as a prison. A king could send people to this prison with no trial. To the French people, the Bastille was a symbol that the king had too much power. Bastille Day is a time to celebrate French unity and culture.

Chapter 3

CULTURE AND PEOPLE

France has a diverse population. Many French people are the descendants of the Indigenous Celts, like the Gauls. Many have other European ancestors. Some French people have Slavic, African, Asian, and Basque ancestors. Many of these people traveled or were brought to France when their countries were colonies of the French colonial empire.

Food

People around the world love French cuisine. Crêpes are a traditional dish in the region of Brittany. These thin, light pancakes are stuffed with sweet filling, such as chocolate. The most popular bread is the baguette. *Baguette* means "stick." These long loaves of bread have crispy crusts and chewy centers. Cheese is also very popular in France. Over three hundred kinds of cheese are made in France. Each region of France has its own cuisine. Butter is used in the north where dairy farms are common. Olive oil is more popular in the south, where olives grow. Restaurants serve seafood on the coast.

Bread on display in a French bakery and pastry shop

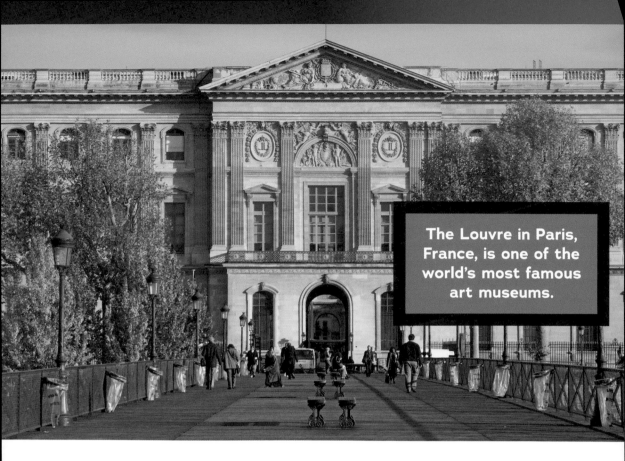

The Louvre in Paris, France, is one of the world's most famous art museums.

Arts

France has a rich art history that dates back to cave paintings in ancient times. Modern French art includes literature, painting, sculpture, music, dance, architecture, photography, and film. The world-famous Cannes Film Festival celebrates the art of filmmaking.

The government provides funding for artists and art programs. Major art exhibits appear in museums in Paris, France's capital and most populous city. French artists study at schools and colleges in Paris and across the country.

Let's Celebrate:
Fête de la Musique

The Fête de la Musique (festival of music) began in 1982 and is celebrated each year on June 21. People play free, live music in France's streets, parks, gardens, storefronts, and more. The festival is not only for professional musicians. Everyone is invited to join and play music. About five million French people have played an instrument or sung in public for the Fête de la Musique.

Religion

France has no official religion. About half of French people practice Christianity, including Roman Catholicism. People also practice other religions in France, such as Islam, Buddhism, and Judaism. About 33 percent of the population is not religious.

Notre Dame Cathedral

Chapter 4

DAILY LIFE

Most of France's population lives in the north and southeast. About 80 percent of people live in cities. Paris is the largest city in France with a population of two million. Other large cities include Lyon, Marseille, and Bordeaux. People who live in these cities have easy access to jobs and entertainment, such as restaurants, museums, and nightlife.

STREET TRAFFIC AT DUSK
IN PARIS, FRANCE
▼

Many people who live in cities take their vacations in the countryside. Other people live in the countryside year-round. People who live in rural France where small farms dot the plains may hear tractors, cowbells, and crowing roosters.

Cows dot the landscape in the Rhône-Alpes region of France.

Tourists enjoy the view near the Eiffel Tower in Paris.

Economy

The French economy depends on tourism. About eighty-nine million foreign tourists visit France each year. It is the most popular tourist destination in the world. The tourism industry includes hotels, restaurants, museums, and transportation. About seven million people visit the Eiffel Tower in Paris each year. Tourists climb the steps or ride the elevators for a beautiful view of Paris. The tower contains restaurants, a dining hall, and gift shops.

While tourism is important in France, other industries are also critical, such as the chemical, textile, and automobile industries. Agriculture is a smaller part of the French economy. Farmers grow wheat, barley, potatoes, grapes, apples, and more. Climate change is affecting French farmers and their crops. Climate change causes higher temperatures and less rainfall. Less rainfall means fewer crops succeed, so farmers have less food to sell.

Businesspeople walk to their offices in Paris's business district.

A mother and her sons root for a French sports team.

Plans for the Future

In September 2020, the French government announced a plan to improve the country's economy. The France Relance is a ten-year plan to increase green energy, conservation, technology, and jobs. The government will spend more than $100 billion to develop these areas. The government hopes that the improvements will attract more people to start businesses and make groundbreaking discoveries in science.

People have lived in France for thousands of years. The people of France are united by a proud history and culture. France has been a world leader for centuries and will continue to lead into the future.

Map and Key Facts

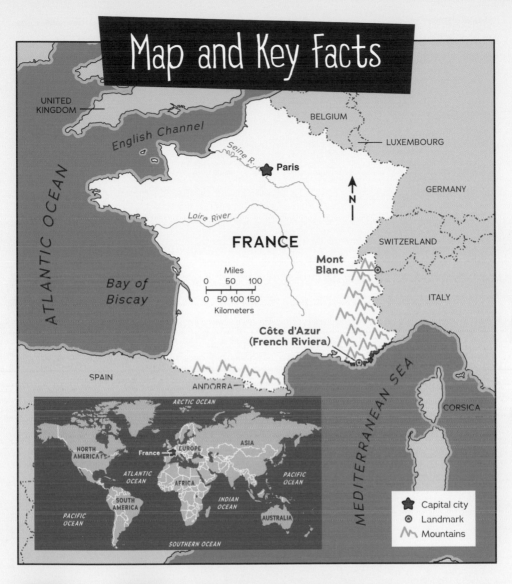

Flag of France

- **Continent: Europe**
- **Capital city: Paris**
- **Population: 68,305,148**
- **Languages: French and many regional languages**

Glossary

ancestor: a member of a family who lived long ago

conservation: the protection of forests, wildlife, and natural resources

cuisine: a style of food

diverse: differing from one another

green energy: energy from renewable sources such as the sun or wind

Indigenous: people who are native to a region

monarchy: a government in which the head of state is a king or queen

republic: a government where the people elect representatives who manage the government

rural: having to do with the countryside, country life, or farming

textile: a woven or knit cloth

Learn More

Britannica Kids: France
    https://kids.britannica.com/kids/article/France/345690

Kids World Travel Guide: France Facts
    https://www.kids-world-travel-guide.com/france-facts.html

Kissock, Heather. *Paris*. New York: AV2, 2022.

National Geographic Kids: France
    https://kids.nationalgeographic.com/geography/countries/article/
    france

Nnachi, Ngeri. *Spotlight on France*. Minneapolis: Lerner Publications,
    2024.

Vonder Brink, Tracy. *Europe*. New York: Crabtree, 2023.

Index

Photo Acknowledgments

Image credits: © Marco Bottigelli/Getty Images, p. 5; Nancy Brown/Getty Images, p. 6; Julian Elliott Photography/Getty Images, p. 7; Pierre Longnus/Getty Images, p. 8; Achim Thomae/ Getty Images, p. 9; Boccalupo Photography/Getty Images, p. 11; Photos.com/Getty Images, p. 12; Artwork by Jean-Pierre Houël, courtesy of Wikimedia Commons, p. 13; Mister_Knight/ Shutterstock, p. 14; Artwork by Jacques-Louis David, courtesy of Wikimedia Commons, p. 15; Valeria Mongelli/Bloomberg/Getty Images, p. 16; DreamSlamStudio/Shutterstock, p. 17; Massimo Borchi/Atlantide Phototravel/Getty Images, p. 19; Walter Bibikow/Getty Images, p. 20; David A. Barnes/Alamy Stock Photo, p. 21; Nikada/Getty Images, p. 22; Loïc Lagarde/ Getty Images, p. 24; Naomi Rahim/Getty Images, p. 25; James O'Neil/Getty Images, p. 26; EschCollection/Getty Images, p. 27; Photo and Co/Getty Images, p. 28.

Cover: Image Source/Getty Images.